Pocket Guides
to the Internet

POCKET GUIDES TO THE INTERNET
BY MARK VELJKOV AND GEORGE HARTNELL

1. TELNETTING
(ISBN 0-88736-943-X)

2. TRANSFERRING FILES WITH FILE TRANSFER PROTOCOL (FTP)
(ISBN 0-88736-944-8)

3. USING AND NAVIGATING USENET
(ISBN 0-88736-945-6)

4. THE INTERNET E-MAIL SYSTEM
(ISBN 0-88736-946-4)

5. BASIC INTERNET UTILITIES
(0-88736-947-2)

6. TERMINAL CONNECTIONS
(0-88736-948-0)

POCKET GUIDES TO THE INTERNET: VOLUME 2:

TRANSFERRING FILES WITH FILE TRANSFER PROTOCOL

Mark Veljkov and George Hartnell

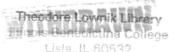
Mecklermedia
WESTPORT • LONDON

Library of Congress Cataloging-in-Publication Data

Veljkov, Mark D.
    Pocket guides to the Internet / Mark Veljkov and George Hartnell.
      p. cm.
    Contents: v. 1. Telnetting -- v. 2. Transferring files with file
transfer protocol (ftp) -- v. 3. Using and navigating Usenet -- v. 4. The
Internet E-mail system -- v. 5. Basic Internet utilities -- v. 6. Terminal
connections
    ISBN 0-88736-943-X (v.1) : $ --ISBN 0-88736-944-8 (v. 2) : $ --
ISBN 0-88736-945-6 (v. 3) : $ -- ISBN 0-88736-946-4 (v. 4) : $ --
ISBN 0-88736-947-2 (v. 5) : $ -- ISBN 0-88736-948-0 (v. 6) : $
    1. Internet (Computer network)--Handbooks, manuals, etc.
I. Hartnell, George, 1949- . II. Title.
TK5105.875.I57V45 1994
004.6'7--dc20   93-40260
                                                                 CIP

British Library Cataloguing-in-Publication Data is available

Mecklermedia, the publishing division of Meckler Corporation,
  11 Ferry Lane West, Westport, CT 06880.
Mecklermedia Ltd., Artillery House, Artillery Row, London SW1P 1RT, UK.

Printed in the United States of America.

CONTENTS

INTRODUCTION

The Internet started with a large U.S. government network called ARPAnet. Today, the Internet has become a worldwide network of networks which interconnects many different computers ranging in size from the Macintosh and IBM-PC to sophisticated mainframes and supercomputers. This network of networks is used for many different purposes. People use the Internet to:

- retrieve free software;
- find and retrieve important documents;
- access library catalogs;
- carry on long distance relationships and conversations with other users;
- conduct research;
- connect to supercomputers; and
- many other activities too numerous to mention.

With all of this interconnecting of computers and networks, the Internet has become huge. In fact, no one is really sure just how big it has become. The Internet is made up of many types of computers, using a variety of operating systems such as DOS, UNIX, or VAX/VMS. These different computers and operating systems can all exchange data by connecting the different computers and computer networks with a standard set of communication procedures called protocols. On the Internet these protocols are called TCP/IP (Transmission Control Protocol/Internet Protocol).

In addition to these TCP/IP communication protocols, there are a variety of operating systems being used to control Internet hosts. The most common is the UNIX operating system which includes variations of UNIX such as XENIX, Apple Computer's A/UX, and IBM's AIX. Not all Internet hosts use UNIX, however. Some hosts utilize the VAX/VMS operating system, DOS, or Macintosh systems. Even though some hosts do not use UNIX, many Internet procedures and applications use commands similar to those empoyed under the UNIX operating system.

Experts have said that information may be the next commodity, and information sources have already become salable items. In the next few years, knowing how to access and retrieve the vast information sources found on the Internet may prove to be one of the most valuable learning experiences you can give yourself.

POCKET GUIDES TO THE INTERNET

Each of the *Pocket Guides to the Internet* is designed to offer you a quick reference guide for connecting to, and navigating through, the Internet. The guides will not only supply you with step-by-step instructions, but each guide will also provide helpful tips, hints, and shortcuts along with a glossary. In addition, some of the guides will provide you with sample Internet addresses for you to use and explore. These guides are not meant to be comprehensive surveys of the Internet. Rather, we hope you will refer to these guides to get you started, to help you through some rough spots, and even possibly to enlighten you. Refer to one of the publications listed at the back of the book for more in-depth information about the Internet.

HOW TO READ THESE GUIDES

These *Guides* all use the same structure when describing the command syntax associated with Internet commands.

Convention	Meaning
an.internet.host	Whatever appears in italics should always be replaced with the appropriate host name.
your-e-mail-address	This command should be replaced with an actual e-mail address.
address, filename, text string	Whatever appears in italics will be replaced with actual information from the host.
--MORE--(nn%)	Whenever you see nn an actual number will be used by the host.
^c,^g,^h, etc.	The ^ is called a Caret (pronounced carrot) and signifies the Control key on your keyboard. A caret with a corresponding letter means that you must hold down the Control key while pressing the corresponding letter.

When you see [enter] following a procedure, you should hit the "enter" or "return" key to effect the procedure. Commands should be entered as shown, with spaces where there are spaces and punctuation exactly as written; otherwise your session may be unsuccessful.

In addition, when you see,

enter this,

q

You should type whatever character(s) appear there and then hit the "enter" or "return" key.

INTERNET PROMPTS

When you first get on to the Internet you can be presented with several different prompts. What these prompts look like will depend on each individual host. In fact, the basic prompt can vary from host to host. Basic Internet prompts include:

- Initial logon prompt.
  Logon prompts are also called **System** or **Host** prompts. These are the prompts you see when you first logon to your local Internet host. The most common Internet logon prompts might look like this:

Prompt	System
%	UNIX/Xenix/A/UX
:	UNIX
>	UNIX
$	VAX/VMS

- Command prompts.
  Command prompts are the prompts you see when you are doing things such as Telnetting or ftp. The most common Internet command prompts might look like this:

```
ftp>
telnet>
    >
```

Your local Internet prompt might even be a **name** of a particular host such as,

```
henson:
```

On some hosts you will see a menu rather than a simple prompt. In our examples, we will not include the local prompt since it is so dependent on your local system.

Internet Addresses

There are three basic Internet addresses you will encounter.

1. Standard Internet e-mail address

```
name@location.more.edu
```

This is the type of addresses you will use primarily for individual e-mail messages. Generally, you do not use these addresses for accessing Internet database information services. Here is an example of an Internet e-mail address.

```
george@henson.cc.wwu.edu
```

The e-mail address consists of three basic parts.

george	This is the user's mail name
@	Stands for the word "at"
henson.cc.wwu.edus	The host where the person's mail box is located

2. Internet host address

```
an.Internet.address
```

The Internet host address consists of three basic parts:

an	Internet	address
host name	subdomain	First level domain

The last part of the address, first level domain, has a unique name that identifies a type of organization. Listed below are the major first level domains of the Internet.

Address	Organization
edu	Educational and research institutions
com	Commercial organizations
gov	Government agencies
mil	Military agencies
net	Major network support centers
org	Other organizations

3. Internet Protocol (IP) Address

The IP address is a numeric address that looks like this:

```
140.160.0.0
```

IP addresses are the same as Internet addresses except that they are in numeric form and the order for identifying hosts is reversed.

140	160	0	0
First level domain	subdomain	subdomain	host name

GETTING HELP WHILE ONLINE

Undoubtedly there will be times when you need will need help when you are online. Help is usually available for most of the commands you will use. You can access help in one of several ways.

1. At the system prompt.
   When you are presented with your system, or host prompt, [i.e., the %, :, >, or $ prompt sign] you can get help on a specific topic or command by typing one of the following commands,

   ```
   help
   command /?
   /h
   ```

In general, typing these commands will bring up a list of help topics valid for the system you are currently in. Once you know the topic, you can enhance your help request by citing a particular topic in your command (remember to substitute an actual term for the italicized *topic* below):

```
man(man  short for manual) topic
help topic
```

2. At a command line prompt.
   When you are presented with your command line prompt [e.g., ftp> or telnet>] you can get help on a specific command or subcommand by typing a question mark. For example,

   ```
   telnet> ? topic
   telnet> topic ?
   ftp> ? topic
   archie> help
   >?
   ```

If there is no response to help or if there is no manual or help entry for your topic, the host will respond with a message similar to,

```
No manual entry for topic
No help available for topic
?Invalid help command topic
```

This usually means that you spelled the topic wrong or picked a topic on which no help is available.

TYPES OF INTERNET CONNECTIONS

There are two main ways to connect to the Internet:

1. Directly-from your desktop computer (PC) or terminal. When you connect directly to an Internet host, your PC or terminal is connected directly to the host. Several popular methods of direct connections are:

    *   through an Ethernet connection
    *   through a direct serial connection
    *   through some other local area network connection
    *   through some combination of the above

Direct connection will allow you to use a variety of utilities that only operate through a direct connection such as Ethernet. These utilities make access and navigating the Internet much faster and easier. TurboGopher, Fetch and NCSA Telnet are examples of utilities that require a direct connection.

2. Remote, through a modem. Many individuals will need to use a modem to connect to an Internet host. There are many brands and speeds of modems for you to select. Which modem you use will depend on your

host. Your host will determine, how many people can connect by modem and at what baud rate (i.e., the speed of modem data transfer).

Depending on the communication software you use, connecting with a modem has several disadvantages. Among them are:

- limited capabilites, such as not being able to send or receive files using File Transfer Protocol (ftp) or other Internet protocols;
- slow communications; and
- slow file transfer.

Check with your system administrator to find out what type of remote connections your host offers.

THIS GUIDE

This guide is targeted toward the Internet's File Transfer Protocol. It will provide you with step-by-step instructions for how to:

- connect to a remote host with anonymous ftp using a sample log on;
- change host directories;
- list the contents of a directory;
- locate a document file; and
- complete a file transfer to your own Internet account.

Chapter 1
What is FTP?

One of the best methods for obtaining data from any network is by using a standard software method for transferring files. The Internet system is no different and provides an application aptly named **File Transfer Protocol.** File Transfer Protocol is most commonly referred to as ftp. In fact, at your Internet system prompt [%, :, >, or $] you will usually use the command ftp to begin your File Transfer Protocol session. Basically, when you ftp you will be copying files from a remote host computer to your Internet account. FTP allows you to share files with other network users, retrieve informative documents for educational purposes, conduct research, and obtain software programs (shareware and public domain) from archives all over the world.

Many host computers on the Internet allow you to freely access a collection of documents and/or programs stored on their computers. Because you do not have to be a registered user of their system to retrieve these files, this type of ftp is commonly referred to as "anonymous ftp." Although anonymous ftp is an excellent way to retrieve files from a remote host, not all systems make files available for anonymous ftp retrieval. To determine whether a host allows anonymous access, you should try to connect to it using the steps described in the next chapter, "How to FTP."

While anonymous ftp is most commonly offered at universities and research institutions, corporations are also beginning to offer anonymous ftp sites. Apple Computer, Inc., and Digital Equipment Corporation (DEC) are two that offer anonymous access to selected files (see "Addresses" at the end of this guide).

Chapter 2
How to FTP

Basic Anonymous FTP Commands

1. The basic command to begin an ftp session is to enter the following at your system prompt,

   ```
   ftp an.Internet.address
   ```

   Remember that you must substitute actual information for the italicized type here.

2. The remote host will respond with,

   ```
   Connected to host.address
   Name <(host.address:your@network.name)>:
   ```

3. At an anonymous ftp site, you will be prompted to type in a name. At this prompt,

   ```
   Name <(host.address:your@network.name)>:
   ```

   enter this,

   ```
   anonymous
   ```

   or,

   ```
   ftp
   ```

4. The remote host will respond with something like,

   ```
   331 Guest login ok, send ident as password.
   Password:
   ```

13

5. At this prompt, type in your Internet e-mail address,

```
Password:
```

enter this,

```
your@Internet.address
```

You will not see your password as you type it in.

Even though most anonymous ftp sites will accept almost anything as a password, it is good etiquette to use your e-mail address. This allows the system administrator to track the usage of their site.

Your Internet address should look something like this,

```
markv@henson.cc.wwu.edu
```

6. After you type in your password, the remote host will respond with something similar to,

```
230 Guest login ok, access restrictions apply
ftp>
```

You are now connected to an ftp site and will see the ftp prompt (ftp>). Throughout your ftp session you will enter the ftp commands at this ftp prompt.

If you have not entered the word anonymous correctly or if you do not enter a password, the host will not allow you to access its files. Although the ftp application is still running, and you are still connected to the host, you will not be able to use other ftp commands. The best way to handle this situation is to type quit at the prompt to return to your local system prompt. You can then try the ftp command again.

7. If you need some help with ftp, at this prompt,

```
ftp>
```

enter this,

```
?
```

Typing a question mark (or the word help) will usually bring up a list of help topics. You can then get help by selecting individual topics from this list. At the prompt,

```
ftp>
```

enter this,

```
? topic name
```

PRACTICE: LOGGING ON TO A REMOTE HOST

To try the anonymous ftp procedures detailed above, let's do a basic connect to an anonymous site.

1. At your system prompt type,

```
ftp ftp.ncsa.uiuc.edu
```

Notice the space after the first ftp. The first ftp is your command to your computer to engage the ftp function. The address ftp.ncsa.uiuc.edu is the address fan ftp site. Not all ftp sites have the letters ftp in their address, however.)

2. The remote host will answer with:

```
Connected to zaphod.ncsa.uiuc.edu.
220 zaphod FTP server (Version 6.23 Thu Apr 8
06:37:40 CDT 1993) ready.
Name (ftp.ncsa.uiuc.edu:markv):
```

3. At this prompt for your name, type,

```
anonymous
```

4. The host will then respond with,

```
331 Guest login ok, send e-mail address as
password.
Password:
```

5. When prompted with Password: type your e-mail address. Your e-mail address should look something like this,

```
markv@henson.cc.wwu.edu
```

You will not see your password as you type it in. This is to protect your privacy.

6. The host will then respond with a lengthy login message and in a few seconds you will see,

```
ftp>
```

This is the standard ftp prompt you see when you have successfully connected to a remote host.

Now that your are connected to an ftp site, let's move on to a discussion of other commands you will need to effectively find and retrieve the files you are looking for.

CHAPTER 3
DIRECTORIES

VIEWING AND CHANGING DIRECTORIES

Internet hosts are a collection of files and these files all have unique names. The files are then organized into **directories** and these directories act as "file cabinets" that store user and system files. Directories are organized in a type of hierarchical file system called a **tree structure**. The tree structure of the Internet file system is shaped like an inverted tree with the base or "**root directory**" at the top and the branches or files and sub directories extending out from the main root directory.

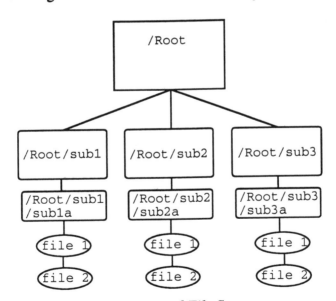

Basic Internet Host Directory and File Structure

Once you have made your connection to an anonymous ftp site you will want to explore what the site has to offer. When you first login you will be in a login directory. The login directory is the first directory you have access to after you login to an anonymous ftp host. From this basic login directory, you can see files and subdirectories to explore. You use ftp commands to view and change to other directories to find the files you want.

Any directory can contain subdirectories which in turn can contain more files. In the language of Internet, subdirectories are often called the "child", and the main directory that holds the subdirectory is aptly named the "parent."

The basic command for viewing directories is ls, short for (list).

```
ftp> ls
```

This command only produces a simple listing of file names. This list will not tell you such information as how big the file is, what kind of file it is, and when the file was last updated.

The following option added to the ls command will give you a listing that is more complete and will provide you with information about your files such as how big the file is, what type of file it is, and when the file was last updated. This option is -l. This is is **not** the number one but is a lower case "l." The full command is short for list -long. Thus,

```
ftp> ls -l
```

You must be sure to include a space between ls and -l.

You can also try the dir (or directory) command at the ftp>. The dir command will return the same listing as the ls -l command. However, not all hosts support the dir command. The ls -l command is more universal.

PRACTICE: VIEWING THE CURRENT DIRECTORY

Once you have connected to an ftp site as explained in Chapter 2, try the following steps to view your current directory.

These examples are from the ftp.ncsa.uiuc.edu site we connected to in the logon practice session.

1. At this prompt,

    ftp>

    enter this,

    ls

2. The remote host then answers with;

```
200 PORT command successful.
150 Opening ASCII mode data connection for file
list.
HDF
Mac
PC
Samples
UNIX
bin
etc
incoming
misc
outgoing
aff
SGI
survey
```

```
ncsapubs
Documentation
DTM
Web
Education
GlobalModels
README_Dialin
INDEX
README.BROCHURE
README.FIRST
ls-lR.Z
README
x3j3
.index
.message
DEC_Alpha
Collage
Mosaic
Telnet
sc22wg5
VR
226 Transfer complete.
286 bytes received in 0.05 seconds (5.6 Kbytes/s)
ftp>
```

This list is not very useful because it does not supply you with much information such as which names represent directories and which names represent files.

3. To get more information about files and directories, at this prompt,

```
ftp>
```

enter this,

```
ls -l
```

4. The remote host then answers with:

```
200 PORT command successful.
150 Opening ASCII mode data connection for /bin/ls.
total 219
-rw-r--r--   1   root    1         989    Oct 12  06:01  .index
-rwxr-xr-x   1   root    1         741    May  4  05:07  .message
drwxr-xr-x   2   root    wheel     512    Oct 12  06:26  Collage
drwxr-xr-x   4   11231   wsstaff   1536   Oct 12  06:25  DEC_Alpha
drwxr-xr-x   4   root    1         512    Feb 12  1993   DTM
drwxrwxr-x  19   root    1         512    Oct 12  06:20  Documentation
drwxrwxr-x   9   11112   571       512    Oct 12  06:21  Education
drwxr-xr-x  12   32766   wsstaff   512    Oct 12  06:24  GlobalModels
drwxrwxr-x   9   10760   wheel     512    Oct 12  06:01  HDF
-rw-r--r--   1   5407    1         46265  Oct 30  08:00  INDEX
drwxr-xr-x  20   root    wheel     512    Oct 12  06:06  Mac
lrwxrwxrwx   1   root    1         3      Apr  1  1993   Mosaic -> Web
drwxr-xr-x  10   root    wheel     512    Oct 12  06:07  PC
-rwxr-xr-x   1   root    wheel     474    Jul 23  1991   README
-rwxr-xr-x   1   root    wheel     25819  Sep 12  1992   README.BROCHURE
-rwxr-xr-x   1   5407    1         16944  Oct  3  22:45  README.FIRST
-rw-r--r--   1   root    1         3081   Sep  2  1992   README_Dialin
drwxr-xr-x   7   10311   wsstaff   512    Oct 12  19:15  SGI
drwxr-xr-x   3   root    wheel     1024   Apr 21  1992   Samples
drwxr-xr-x   2   root    1         512    Oct 12  06:26  Telnet
drwxr-xr-x  17   root    wheel     512    Oct 12  06:07  UNIX
drwxr-xr-x   4   5029    wsstaff   512    Oct 12  06:26  VR
drwxr-xr-x  15   11811   wsstaff   512    Oct 12  06:20  Web
drwxr-xr-x  10   loric   wheel     512    Apr 21  1992   aff
drwxr-x--x   2   root    wheel     512    Oct 30  06:02  bin
drwxr-xr-x   5   root    wsstaff   512    Oct 12  06:08  etc
drwxr-xr-x  59   root    wsstaff   1536   Oct 12  06:08  incoming
-rw-r--r--   1   root    1         95025  Jul 21  15:14  ls-lR.Z
drwxr-xr-x  10   root    wheel     512    Oct 12  06:13  misc
drwxrwxr-x  18   root    552       512    Oct 30  06:04  ncsapubs
drwxr-xr-x  75   root    other     1536   Oct 12  06:13  outgoing
drwxr-xr-x   3   221     1         512    Oct 12  06:26  sc22wg5
drwxr-xr-x   2   root    1         512    Apr 21  1992   survey
drwxrwxr-x   4   221     552       1536   Oct 12  06:25  x3j3
226 Transfer complete.
2140 bytes received in 2.4 seconds (0.86 Kbytes/s)
ftp>
```

This is the listing of the login (root) directory of the host
ftp.ncsa.uiuc.edu. While this listing still looks quite
cryptic, it does contain more additional information (more than
using just the -ls command) about the files and directories
that are stored on this host.

ANATOMY OF AN INTERNET DIRECTORY LISTING

Now that you have listed your directory, you will need an idea of what you are looking at. Using a sample line from the above listing, the breakdown of the listing structure looks like this:

```
1           2  3     4      5    6       7      8
drwxr-xr-x 2   root  wheel  512  Oct 12  06:26  Collage
```

COLUMN 1- drwxr-xr-x
This column represents file type and permissions. It is the first character that is the most important to you as an ftp user.

The first character tells you the "type" of file referred to in the list. That is, if this is a file or a directory.

  d = directory of files
  - = regular file
  l= a linked name

A linked name is an alias file or directory linked to an actual other file or directory located somewhere else on this host.

The remaining characters stand for user permissions. These characters determine the type and amount of access that an end user has. If you want more information on the meaning of these characters you may wish to refer to one of the many books on the UNIX operating system.

COLUMNS 2, 3, & 4
These columns provide file identity information not important to the ftp process.

COLUMN 5- `512`
This is the default size (in bytes) for directory information or file size. When a directory is created on an Internet host, the host allocates a certain number of bytes to maintain basic information about the directory. This number does not refer to the size of the directory itself.

COLUMN 6- `Oct 12`
This is the directory or files modification/creation date. All Internet directories and files are date stamped. Any modification by any users results in a new date (and time) being stamped on the file. You can use this column to see the age of the file you might be trying to access.

COLUMN 7- `06:26`
This is the modification/creation time. In addition to date stamping, all Internet directories and files are time stamped. Any modification by any users results in a new time (and date) being stamped on the file.

COLUMN 8- `Collage`
The final column is the actual name of the directory or file.

The rest of the information `226 Transfer complete.` `2140 bytes received in 2.4 seconds (0.86 Kbytes/s) ftp` simply tells you that the remote host has sent the requested information (directory listing or file) in a text format. This is all part of the connection process.

CHANGING DIRECTORIES

You will want to list the files and directories when you first connect to an anonymous ftp site. This allows you to view what directories are available for you to explore. Changing directories

allows you to select a directory that looks interesting to you and
to view the files (or other directories) that are in the directory.

At the `ftp` prompt, the basic command to change directories is
cd (short for **change** directory),

```
ftp> cd <directory name>
```

After changing directories, you will want to see what files are
available by entering the basic command for viewing directories,

```
ftp> ls -l
```

or

```
ftp> dir
```

With these commands, `ls -l`, `dir`, and cd, you can navi-
gate through the directories of files located at an ftp site.

PRACTICE: CHANGING DIRECTORIES

1. Using our connection to `ftp.ncsa.uiuc.edu`, at this
   prompt,

   ```
   ftp>
   ```

   enter this,

   ```
   ls -l
   ```

This brings up the listing shown on page 21. The fragment below repeats the end of that list of files and directories you have
access to.

```
-rw-r--r--   1   root  1      95025  Jul 21  15:14    ls-lR.Z
drwxr-xr-x  10   root  wheel  512    Oct 12  06:13    misc
drwxrwxr-x  18   root  552    512    Oct 30  06:04    ncsapubs
drwxr-xr-x  75   root  other  1536   Oct 12  06:13    outgoing
drwxr-xr-x   3   221   1      512    Oct 12  06:26    sc22wg5
drwxr-xr-x   2   root  1      512    Apr 21  1992     survey
drwxrwxr-x   4   221   552    1536   Oct 12  06:25    x3j3
226 Transfer complete.
2140 bytes received in 2.4 seconds (0.86 Kbytes/s)
ftp>
```

If you are confused as to which directory to start with, try the directory called ncsapubs (remember that the extreme right hand column shows the name of each file in the list). You will find files called pub at many ftp sites. These are usually a good starting point for general information and files.

2. Change to the ncsapubs directory. At this prompt,

```
ftp>
```

enter this,

```
cd ncsapubs
```

This takes you to the directory called ncsapubs.

3. To list the files in this directory, at this prompt,

```
ftp>
```

enter this,

```
ftp> ls -l
```

The host will now display the contents of the new directory ncsapubs.

```
200 PORT command successful.
150 Opening ASCII mode data connection for /bin/ls.
total 121
-rw-rw-rw-   1 9846   552   6900  Oct  7 13:04  .HSancillary
-rw-r--r--   1 root   1     724   Oct 31 06:04  .index
drwxrwxr-x   2 13676  552   512   Oct 31 06:04  AFS
drwxrwxr-x   2 12042  10    512   Oct 31 06:04  ApplicationInfo
drwxr-xr-x   2 13676  552   512   Oct 12 06:20  CM_Guide
drwxrwxr-x   2 13676  552   512   Oct 12 06:20  ConvexGuide
drwxrwxr-x   2 5504   10    512   Oct 12 06:20  InfoPacket93
drwxrwxr-x   2 12042  552   512   Oct 31 06:04  MetaCenter
drwxrwxr-x   2 2684   552   512   Oct 12 06:19  Misc
drwxr-xr-x   2 12042  552   512   Feb 12 1993   NSFinformation
-rw-rw-r--   1 13676  552   3612  Sep 14 21:01  README
drwxrwxr-x   2 2684   552   512   Feb 12 1993   ReferenceCard
drwxrwxr-x   2 2684   552   512   Feb 12 1993   ResBiblio
-rw-r--r--   1 5504   10    14342 Aug 16 20:26  SoftwareListing
drwxrwxr-x   2 2684   552   512   Oct 12 06:20  SystemIntro
-rw-r--r--   1 5504   10    65537 Sep 28 15:21  TechResCatalog
drwxrwxr-x   2 13676  552   512   Oct 12 06:20  UniTree
drwxrwxr-x   5 326    552   512   Oct 12 06:20  access
-rw-r--r--   1 5504   10    12351 Oct 15 20:48  calendar
drwxrwxr-x   6 2476   552   512   Oct 12 06:19  datalink
drwxrwxr-x   7 2684   552   1024  Oct 12 06:19  preprints
drwxrwxr-x   2 2476   552   512   Oct 12 06:19  startup
226 Transfer complete.
1451 bytes received in 1.4 seconds (1 Kbytes/s)
ftp>
```

As you can see, there are many more directories (d) for you to explore. Continue to use the cd command to explore each of these directories.

MOVING UP IN THE DIRECTORIES

As you explore the various directories you will find there are directories inside of directories. Once you move into a subdirectory you are no longer at the directory you started in when you first connected. You will eventually want to go back and look at the directories you came from. There are several commands you can type at `ftp>` that allow you to back up to the previous directory.

    cdup

or,

    cd *directory name* **(You must include a space between cd and the directory name)**

If you want to go all the way back to the login (root) directory type,

    cd / **(You must include a space between cd and the /)**

A word of caution here. This may look like the backslash (\) used in DOS (the operating system of IBM and compatible personal computers). It is not the same! The backslash in DOS (\) is the opposite of the / used to move back to the login directory in ftp.

PRACTICE: MOVING UP IN THE DIRECTORIES

Still using our connection to `ftp.ncsa.uiuc.edu` we can practice moving back a directory.

1. At this prompt,

       ftp>

   enter this,

       cdup

   or,

       cd *directory name*

These commands will move you back up to the directory you just came from.

2. Now you can view the directory you are currently in. At this prompt,

    ```
    ftp>
    ```

    enter this,

    ```
    ls -l
    ```

As you can see, you are now back to the previous directory (the one you were in before you changed to the ncsapubs directory).

LEAVING THE REMOTE HOST

To quit the ftp application and leave the remote host, you use the quit command. You can use quit at any time during your ftp session by typing quit at the ftp prompt.

```
ftp> quit
```

This will take you back to your own local system prompt.

PRACTICE: QUITTING AN FTP SESSION

Still using the connection to ftp.ncsa.uiuc.edu use the quit command to quit the ftp application and end your connection with ftp.ncsa.uiuc.edu

1. At this prompt,

   ```
   ftp>
   ```

   enter this,

   ```
   quit
   ```

2. The host will respond with,

   ```
   221 Goodbye.
   ```

You should now find yourself back at your system prompt.

CHAPTER 4
FILES

TRANSFERRING FILES WITH FTP-
FILE TYPES

There are two basic types of files you will want to get from a remote Internet host.

1. ASCII FILES (TEXT)

ASCII stands for **American Standard Code for Information Interchange**. ASCII files are more commonly called "text" files. More specifically, they are "text-only" files which means they have not been saved in the file format of the application that created them. For example, if you create a letter in the word processing program WordPerfect, you can save your letter as a WordPerfect file or, you can also save the letter as a text-only (ASCII) file. ASCII files are not applications such as utility programs or games.

2. BINARY FILES (PROGRAMS, NON-TEXT FILES)

Binary files are applications or files that have been saved in the format of the application that created them. Binary files can be any of the following and more.

- applications
- utilities
- word processing documents
- games
- pictures
- sounds

Many binary files are often saved as archived and/or compressed files. Archived files are a collection of related files that have been compressed into a single, large file. You will need a special utility program to "unarchive" these files. These archived files often look like a text-only file to the computer. However, when you use the appropriate unarchive utility program they will become binary files.

Compressed files are large files that have been compressed to a smaller size to make their storage smaller and transfer quicker. Like archived files, compressed files require a special utility program on your Macintosh or MS-DOS computer to "uncompress" them. These utility programs are available on the Internet (see "Addresses" at the end of this book).

You can usually tell the type of file you are transferring by the name of the file extension. The file extension is the last three letters of a file name after the period. Often, ASCII text files will have no extensions at all, such as the typical README file. If a file has no extension, you can assume it is an ASCII or text-only file. Archived and compressed files also have unique extensions.

Here are some examples of files from the ncsa directory showing file extentions:

(These are Mac Files from the directory Mosaic [Path = cd Mosaic\Mac]:

```
-rw-r--r-- 1 9328 wsstaff 2850    Nov 11 01:55  NCSAMosaic.1.0.README
-rw-r--r-- 1 9328 wsstaff 663696 Nov 11 01:54  NCSAMosaicMac.10.sit
```

(Thes are DOS Files from the directory Mosaic [Path = cd Mosaic\Win-dows]:

```
-rw-r--r--   1  9396   wsstaff  240175   Nov 11  21:57  wmos1_0.zip
```

Since you will find many types of files with or without extensions, you can use the following chart as a guide.

Extension	Type	Binary-Text	Utility Needed
None	Text documents	Text	None
.doc	Document	Text	None
.txt	Document	Text	None
.ARC	Archive/Compression	Binary	DOS–arc602
			Mac–ArcMac
.ZIP	PKZIP-Archive/	Binary	DOS–pkz110eu
	Compression		Mac–UnZip
.sit	StuffIt-Archive/	Binary	DOS—unsit30
	Compression		Mac–StuffItLite
.Z	compress	Binary	DOS–u16
			Mac–MacCompress
.pit	PackIt-Archive/	Binary	DOS–UnPackIt
	Compression		Mac–PackIt
.tar	Tape Archive-Archive/	Binary	DOS–tar
	Compression		Mac–UnTar
Hqx	BinHex-Archive	Text	DOS–xbin23
			Mac–BinHex
.gif	Graphical Interchange	Binary	None
	Format		
.sea	Self-extracting	Binary	None
	Archives		

TRANSFERRING FILES WITH FTP–SETTING FILE TYPE

Internet hosts are set by default to transfer all files as ASCII (text). This means that binary files (programs) will be transferred as text files and will not work when you try to run them unless you identify them as such before you transfer them.

Therefore, in order to get binary files from an Internet host you must use ftp to tell the host you are in a binary transfer mode.

1. To go to the binary transfer mode, at this prompt,

    ```
    ftp>
    ```

    enter this,

    ```
    binary
    ```

The Internet host will respond with,

```
200 Type set to I
```

The "I" indicates binary transfer mode. You are now in the binary transfer mode and can transfer binary files successfully.

When you are not sure what format a file is in, transfer to binary mode **before** you use the get command (detailed below). The binary mode will allow you transfer both binary AND text files.

2. To go back to ASCII mode, at this prompt,

    ```
    ftp>
    ```

    enter this,

    ```
    ascii
    ```

The Internet host will respond with,

```
200 Type set to A.
```

You are now back in the ASCII transfer mode.

THE GET COMMAND

The basic command to transfer a file from a remote Internet host to your own Internet account, is `get`. To transfer a file from a host, at the prompt,

```
ftp>
```

enter this,

```
get file.name
```

The Internet is **VERY** literal and case sensitive when it comes to files names! You must type the file name **exactly** as it appears in the directory listing.

PRACTICE: TRANSFERRING AN ASCII TEXT FILE

For this example we will reconnect to `ftp.ncsa.uiuc.edu`.

1. From your system prompt ftp to `ftp.ncsa.uiuc.edu`:

   ```
   ftp ftp.ncsa.uiuc.edu
   ```

2. Type `anonymous` for your login name.

3. Type your Internet e-mail address for you password. Remember, your e-mail address should look something like this,

   ```
   george@henson.cc.wwu.edu
   ```

In a few seconds you will see the `ftp>`.

4. At this prompt,

    ```
    ftp>
    ```

    enter this,

    ```
    ls -l
    ```

This shows you the listing on page 20 which lists the files and directories you have access to. We will use a fragment of this screen below.

```
-rwxr-xr-x   1    5407    1         16944   Oct 3   22:45   README.FIRST
-rw-r--r--   1    root    1         3081    Sep 2   1992    README_Dialin
drwxr-xr-x   7    10311   wsstaff   512     Oct 12  19:15   SGI
drwxr-xr-x   3    root    wheel     1024    Apr 21  1992    Samples
drwxr-xr-x   2    root    1         512     Oct 12  06:26   Telnet
drwxr-xr-x   17   root    wheel     512     Oct 12  06:07   UNIX
drwxr-xr-x   4    5029    wsstaff   512     Oct 12  06:26   VR
```

5. Before you get a text file, make sure you are in the ASCII (text-only) transfer mode by using the ASCII command. By default, most systems start you in the ASCII mode. However, using the ASCII command ensures you are in the text-only transfer mode. At this prompt,

    ```
    ftp>
    ```

    enter this,

    ```
    ascii
    ```

In a few minutes you will see the following response from the host,

    ```
    200 Type set to A.
    ```

You are now in ASCII transfer mode.

6. You will get the text file entitled README.FIRST by using the get command. At this prompt,

```
ftp>
```

enter this,

```
get README.FIRST
```

Be sure to spell this file **exactly** as it appears in the directory. Remember, too, to insert a space between the get command and the file name, README.FIRST. In this case the file name is in all caps. How long it takes for you to successfully "get" the file depends on a number of factors, including the speed of your Internet connection and the amount of traffic on the Internet at the time. You will get a confirmation of a successful transfer of the file. It will be something like,

```
226 Transfer complete.
local: wmos1_0.zip remote:  wmos1_0.zip
241342 bytes received in 82 seconds (2.9 Kby-
tes/s)
ftp>
```

The file README.FIRST is now in one of two locations. This file is either on your local host or your own PC depending on how you are connected to the Internet.

If the README.FIRST file is still on your local host and not your own PC, then you will need to use the appropriate file transfer procedure such as the procedure you use to download your daily mail, to get the file from your local host to your desktop PC.

PRACTICE: TRANSFERRING A BINARY FILE

For this practice session we will stay with our connection to `ftp.ncsa.uiuc.edu`.

1. Make sure you are at your login (root) directory. If you are not sure, at this prompt,

   ```
   ftp>
   ```

   enter this,

   ```
   cd /
   ```

2. Now list your directory. At this prompt,

   ```
   ftp>
   ```

   enter this,

   ```
   ls -l
   ```

3. The full directory is the same as that shown on page 21. Again, here is a brief section of the list.

```
drwxrwxr-x 18 root 552     512 Oct 30 06:04 ncsapubs
drwxr-xr-x 75 root other 1536 Oct 12 06:13 outgoing
drwxr-xr-x 3  221  1       512 Oct 12 06:26 sc22wg5
drwxr-xr-x 2  root 1       512 Apr 21 1992  survey
drwxrwxr-x 4  221  552    1536 Oct 12 06:25 x3j3
226 Transfer complete.
2140 bytes received in 2.4 seconds (0.86 Kbytes/s)
ftp>
```

4. Since there are many files available at most ftp sites, use the change directory command to explore the directories that in-

terest you. For example, change to the directory Mosaic. There you will find directories leading to both Macintosh and Windows versions of the binary file Mosaic. Change directories again to the Mac directory and you will see a listing for the Macintosh version of the file Mosaic. It looks like this,

```
-rw-r--r-- 1 9328 wsstaff 663696 Nov 11 01:54 NCSAMosaicMac.10.sit.hqx
```

Generally, files that end with hqx are Macintosh files, while files that end with zip are IBM files.

5. Before you get a binary file, make sure you are in the binary transfer mode by using the binary command. By default, most systems start you in the ASCII mode. So, to transfer a binary file you need to set the ftp host to binary transfer mode. At this prompt,

```
ftp>
```

enter this,

```
binary
```

In a few minutes you will see the following response from the host,

```
200 Type set to I.
```

You are now in binary transfer mode.

6. Now you can get whichever binary file you like with the get command. At this prompt,

```
ftp>
```

enter this,

```
get NCSAMosaicMac.10.sit.hqx
```

Remember the file named `NCSAMosaicMac.10.sit.hqx` is a Macintosh file and will not work on your IBM.

You will soon get a confirmation that the file has been successfully transferred to your Internet account. The file you transferred is now in one of two locations. The file is either on your local host or your own microcomputer depending on how you are connected to the Internet.

If the file is still on your local host and not your own PC, then you will need to use the appropriate file transfer procedure to get the file from your local host to your desktop PC.

7. When you have finished transferring files you can quit your session with the `quit` command. At this prompt,

```
ftp>
```

enter this,

```
quit
```

You will now be at your system prompt.

VIEWING TEXT FILES ON YOUR SCREEN

You can view the files you transferred with the |more command. The character | is called a "pipe" and allows the file to be displayed on your screen one page at a time. To view your transferred document, at this prompt,

```
ftp>
```
enter this,

```
get filename |more
```

The contents of the file will appear on your screen one page at a time. To display the next page of text, press your spacebar.

When the file contents have finished scrolling, you will be put back at the ftp prompt.

THE BASIC FTP SESSION

What you want to do	What you type
1. To start an ftp session	`ftp host.address`

2. Identify yourself to the host:
    login name:
    password:
	
	`anonymous` (or `ftp`)
	`your@Internet.address`

3. Get help general help: Get help for a specific topic :	`?` `? topic`
4. List the contents of a directory	`ls -l` (or `dir`)
5. Change directories	`cd name of the directory`
6. Move back to the last directory	`cdup` (or `cd /`)
7. To change transfer modes	`ascii` (for text files) `binary` (for binary files)
8. To get a file	`get file.name`
9. To change a file name	`get file.name` `NewFile.NewName`
10. To view a text file on your screen	`get |more`
11. To quit an ftp session	`quit`

BASIC FTP COMMANDS

Command	Meaning
get	gets the specified file and downloads it to your or your host's computer.
ascii	sets the transfer mode for the transfer of an ASCII text file
binary	sets the transfer mode for the transfer of an executable program such as an application, graphics, or sound file
ftp	file transfer protocol command
ls	lists the current directory in short form
ls -l	lists the current directory in long form
cdup	changes directories up; moves back to the previous directory level
?	asks for help
? topic	asks for help on a specific topic
get |more	prints text files to your screen one screen at a time.
quit	quits your ftp session
cd	changes directories
dir	shows the contents of the current directory

GLOSSARY

address The address is your network name or your host computer's name. Everyone connected to the Internet has an address. There are three basic types of Internet address:

1. Host address: *an.internet.address*
2. E-mail address: *name@internet.host.domain*
3. IP address: *123.456.23.8*

anonymous ftp site A computer on the Internet that allows public access to its services through file transfer protocol (ftp).

Archie An Internet system for locating files that are publicly available by anonymous ftp or Telnet.

ARPAnet This is the original experimental U.S. Government network that started the Internet. ARPAnet was started in the 1970's and is no longer in existence.

ASCII Pronounced As-Key. Stands for the American Standards Code for Information Interchange. ASCII is a textual method for representing computer characters.

binary files These are files that are non-ASCII and often represent executable applications and non-textual information such as graphics and sound, word processor text, etc.

client A computer relying on the resources of a host computer.

command line The point at which you enter a command to initiate an action by the computer.

directory An index of files and subdirectories stored on the host.

directory services A service that can provide network addresses and/or userids of hosts, services, and individuals.

e-mail Electronic mail messages sent or received by a person or computer on a computer network.

e-mail address A specific, locateable electronic address that designates a person or service at a specific network site. A standard Internet e-mail address looks like this: name@internet.host.domain.

file transfer protocol (ftp) A standard software protocol that governs the error-corrected transmission of computer data.

gateway A computer that connects two or more networks using different communication standards.

Gopher Software that presents in menu form information found all over the Internet. Gopher programs also allow searches on the Internet for hosts, directories, or files based on keywords supplied by the user.

host The main computer system to which users are connected.

Internet A group of interconnected networks of computers throughout the world.

Internet address A specific address in the form an.internet.address that is assigned to the hosts and services found on the Internet. This is also called a Fully Qualified Domain Name.

listing A list of the what files and directories are available on a host computer.

login To key-in the commands to begin your session with a host.

log on To connect to a host system.

mailbox A file or directory on the end user's host computer that holds the end user's e-mail.

mainframe/minicomputer A large, multi-user, multi-tasking computer that is used by many Internet hosts.

PC A Personal Computer or microcomputer. The Apple Macintosh and the IBM PS/2 are examples of personal computers. Many Internet users use PCs to connect to Internet hosts.

prompt The symbol that appears on your screen informing you that the host is ready to accept your input.

protocols The set of specific communication standards that allow one computer to interact with other computers.

remote host A host computer that is not your host.

root directory The primary directory from which all other directories branch.

self extracting archives A collection of files archived into a single file. Self extracting archives do not need a separate program to unarchive them; they uncompress themselves upon opening.

server An Internet-based computer providing services and information.

shareware Computer software that is sold by requesting that users submit donations to the software developer. Shareware software is not free.

sub directory A directory inside another directory. Sometimes called a Child Directory.

TCP/IP Abbreviation for Transmission Control Protocol/ Internet Protocol. TCP/IP is a set of computer commands that dictate how the computers on the Internet will communicate with each other.

Telnet A standard Internet service that allows users to log on to remote host computers.

terminal The computer used to connect to a host. The terminal can be a personal computer such as a Macintosh, IBM, or compatible microcomputer.

upload To send a file to a remote host or other Internet address.

UNIX A multi-user, multitasking operating system upon which many Internet communication structures are built.

Veronica An additional Gopher service that allows you to do a keyword search of Gopher menus.

WAIS Wide-Area Information Servers, client/server-based databases searchable using common language search terms.

WorldWideWeb WWW, a hypermedia information retrieval system linking a wide range of Internet-accessible documents and data files.

Xenix Pronounced "Zee-nicks". An operating system developed by Microsoft that conforms to UNIX standards and operates on IBM PCs.

ADDRESSES

The following are just some sample address that support anonymous ftp logins. Try them out and see what is there.

`ftp.apple.com`
This is Apple's anonymous ftp site. The host includes some Apple sys-
tem software (like QuickTime 1.0 and 1.5) and other Macintosh related
files.
Login: `anonymous` or `ftp`
Password: `guest`

`ames.arc.nasa.gov`
This originates from NASA's Ames Research Center. It contains Macin-
tosh and IBM files. In addition, it also holds frequently Asked Questions
about space and space exploration.
Login: `anonymous` or `ftp`
Password: `You@internet.address`
`ftp> cd pub/SPACE/FAQ`

`prep.ai.mit.edu`
This site is the Free Software Foundation. Excellent resource for free
software.
Login: `anonymous` or `ftp`
Password: `You@internet.address`
`ftp> cd pub/gnu`

`gatekeeper.dex.com`
Digital Equipment Corporation site. This site also contains
many tasty recipes.
Login: `anonymous` or `ftp`
Password: `You@internet.address`
`ftp> cd pub/recipes`

`wuarchive.wustl.edu`
Electronic versions of *PC Magazine* and an excellent resource for Macintosh, IBM, Amiga, Apple IIe, and Atari programs. In addition, there are games and utilities.
Login: anonymous or `ftp`
Password: `You@internet.address`
`ftp> cd mirrors/msdos/pcmag`

`ra.msstate.edu`
This is the National Archive's Center for Electronic Records.
Login: anonymous or `ftp`
Password: `You@internet.address`
`ftp> cd docs/history`

`boombox.micro.umn.edu`
This is an excellent repository for Gopher client software.
Login: anonymous or `ftp`
Password: `You@internet.address`

`iuvax.cs.indiana.edu`
Aikido dojo list.
Login: anonymous or `ftp`
Password: `You@internet.address`
`ftp> cd pub/aikido`

`coe.montana.edu`
Star Trek archive with a tremendous amount of information related to the various Star Trek series.
Login: anonymous or `ftp`
Password: `You@internet.address`
`ftp> cd pub/STARTREK`

`nic.ddn.mil`
This is a valuable Network Information Center and is worth exploring for a variety of Internet-related data files.
Login: anonymous
Password: `guest`

FOR FURTHER READING

Here is a brief and selective list of books dealing with the Internet. The reader of this *Pocket Guide* may want to read one or more of these books to receive a more comprehensive grounding in Internet concepts as well as to understand the overall context of the specific functions discussed in this book.

Dern, Daniel P. *The Internet Guide for New Users.* New York, NY: McGraw-Hill, Inc., 1993, 570pp.

Gibbs, Mark and Richard Smith. *Navigating the Internet.* Carmel, IN: SAMS Publishing, 1993, 500pp.

Gilster, Paul. *The Internet Navigator.* New York, NY: John Wiley & Sons, Inc., 470pp.

Engle, Mary E. Marilyn Lutz, Williams W. Jones, Jr., and Genevieve Engel. *Internet Connections: A Librarian's Guide to Dial-Up Access and Use.* Chicago, IL: American Library Association, 1993, 166pp.

Krol, Ed. *The Whole Internet User's Guide & Catalog.* Sebastopol, CA: O'Reilly & Associates, Inc., 1992, 376pp.

Lane, Elizabeth and Craig Summerhill. *Internet Primer for Information Professionals.* Westport, CT: Mecklermedia, 1993, 182pp.

LaQuey, Tracy with Jeanne C. Ryer. *The Internet Companion.* Reading, MA: Addison-Wesley Publishing Company, 1993, 196pp.

McClure, Charles R., ed. *Libraries and the Internet/NREN.* Westport, CT: Mecklermedia, 1994, 500pp.

Newby, Gregory B. *Directory of Directories on the Internet.* Westport, CT: Mecklermedia, 1993, 186pp.

Greg R. Notess, *Internet Access Providers: An International Resource Directory.* Westport, CT: Mecklermedia, 1994, 230pp.

On Internet 1994: An International Title and Subject Guide to Electronic Journals, Newsletters, Texts, Discussion Lists, and Other Resources on the Internet. Westport, CT: Mecklermedia, 1993, 600pp.

Tennant, Roy, John Ober, and Anne G. Lipow. *Crossing the Internet Threshold: An Instructional Handbook.* San Carlos, CA: Library Solutions Press, 1993, 134pp.

INDEX

INTERNET Research

Electronic Networking Applications and Policy

Edited by Charles McClure, INTERNET RESEARCH
is the only journal that publishes refereed articles dealing
with the Internet and electronic networking applications.

The contents of a recent issue follow:

- *NFSnet Privatization: Policy Making in a Public Interest Vacuum*

- *The Architecture of a Massively Distributed Hypermedia System*

- *Grace: A System to Support the Development and Issue of Global Computer-Supported Cooperative Work (CSCW) Applications*

- *Must Invisible Colleges Be Invisible? An Approach to Examining Large Communities of Network Users*

- *Assessing Information on the Internet: Toward Providing Library Services for Computer-Mediated Communication*

- *Resource Reviews*

Published quarterly • $115

ISSN: 1066-2243

On Internet 1994

An International Guide to Electronic Journals, Newsletters, Texts, Discussion Lists, and Other Resources on the Internet

Scholarly and commercial electronic publishing over the Internet
and other linked networks has exploded over the last two years.
Recent estimates put the number of discrete publications and discussion
lists available to the searcher at well over 6,000. This annual
directory offers a guide to the full range of electronic documents
currently available, complete with access, subscription, and submission
instructions, descriptive information, listings of contents, reviews,
and indexes to enable users to easily locate publications
of professional and personal interest.

ISSN
1066-9973

$45.00
£29.50 paper

ISBN
0-88736-929-4

500pp.
November
1993

5%
standing
order
discount
available